Table of Contents

Revelation for Marriages

My Perfect Rib

Kone Mphela

Chapter 1

Palesa was doing her master in Psychology and Bongani was candidate Attorney.

One day Palesa came to her father to inform him that she met a man who proposed to her, her father ask "Did you accept?" She said not yet I wanted to talk to you about it first. Her father asks who that man is. She said is Tony my brother 's friend and business associates, her father looked at her and said no, you are not going to accept that proposal, why she asks? And her father said, Tony is not a marriage type man, his life philosophy and norms are not in line. So forget about him and look for someone else if you believe that you are ready for a marriage, but whoever you will present before me, it must be a man.

I know Tony enough to know that the woman he will marry, she will be forever in tears. His family foundation is weak and it will take a miracle and his willingness to rebuild it. However, because of his pride and greed that might never happen, it takes a real man to acknowledge his shortcomings and lack of principles and Tony is certainly not that man, his pride is his biggest weakness and there is no such thing called "once we are married, I will change him and lead him to Christ", if his adulthood didn't change him, then no one can, and that is not your duty as a wife in a marriage, your duty is to be obedient and respect your husband and how can a child of the living God be obedient to a Ritualist.

And I won't allow that marriage to take place because the day his cultist gods or leaders start demanding human blood for ritual sacrifices he is going to take my grandchildren, so it will be my next generation whose life is going to be in danger.

Palesa father left to attend his business meeting and it so happens that he is going to see Bongani father.

Bongani as well he was at home for weekend to introduce his fiancé to his parent and they too didn't accept his choice but didn't tell him but allowed him to spend a weekend and left.

When getting there Palesa father was shocked to see long faces and when he ask, they told him that their son is about to commit the mistake of the worst kind.

How do you mean? He asks, they told him that their son just left with a girl whom he said is going to be his wife and she doesn't look like the obedient type of a girl and she believe in Satanism.

Eish it feels like, this is a plague that is about to fall on every family, is like a curse that was written in the book of Deuteronomy 28:32 said Palesa's father.

In my house I was just talking to my daughter who said she want to get married to the worse kind of a man, yes, he is tall, handsome, educated and also very rich, however, he is not capable of committing or loving anyone, hell he can't even love himself, his definition of love starts with money and end with money. So marrying someone like that is like marrying money and money is a lousy husband but a good servant.

So what did you say to your daughter? They ask.

I told her that she should look somewhere else and forget about Tony.

I set her down and ask her to look for the man who will be more to her like Abraham to Sarah.

It wasn't difficult for Sarah to adore and respect Abraham, yes, he wasn't a perfect man because he once try to prostitute her, but because Abraham was keeping a good company, his friend Almighty God came to his rescue every time he was making some dump decision out of fear.

No man is perfect, but if God is your righteousness like he was to Abraham his Friend, that man is more likely to become a good husband not by his effort but through Christ his right standing.

In my house I have 2 children who are married and their marriage is just a shame, I allowed them to make their choice and to make their own mistakes, but now they are suffering in their marriage, my son spends more time in my house than in his own house because his wife has developed some funny habit and he also said he is haunted, we tried to intervene but we couldn't as his wife beliefs, values and morals are so different to ours, she rather takes advices on a comic book about marriage than listen to us. God to her is like a motivational speaker who makes people feel good. My 1st daughter as well, she eats and sleep sorrows in her marriage. And all these people were financially successful, but because of their failing marriages, their finances is slowly but surely becoming a downward sparrow. Can you imagine that both of my children almost got divorced? It was only by the grace of God that they listen to us when we ask them to give God a chance to rectify what is wrong in their marriages. Even now is still a constant prayer after prayer for them, For God to see them through.

So this one thing I will allow her to go and be a trophy wife again to Tony, she has another thing coming, I will only bless her marriage if she finds a good man, I ask her to choose between these two types of marriage mine and her mom or her sister and brother kind of marriage and she chose mine, I therefore told her that for you to have what we have, you should do what we did.

Bongani's father added by saying, children of this day are not as we were when we grew up, in my time it was my father who introduced a girl for me to marry.

We dated for a few weeks, then we got married, yes, it wasn't easy as I was in a serious relationship at that time and I also hoped to marry the girl of my dreams, my childhood friend, and on the other hands my wife here, he pointed at his wife Bongani's mom, was also in a relationship, but despite all that our parents still forced us to marry, he sighs, come to think of it the day my wife was brought to my house she look like a sheep going to the slaughter, they both laughed, Bongani's parents.

She had to obey her father, regardless and also out of respect to my father I married her.

It wasn't easy because we spend years of our marriage resenting each other, we were both determined not to make it work just to prove a point to our parents, that their backward tradition or believes, was outdated and not working anymore.

So as I live with my wife who was more of a house mate than a wife to me, I continued to see my girlfriend, sometime I will bring her to my house while my wife was in the house, with the aim of annoying her so that she can call off the marriage.

But our parents didn't allow her, she even tried to kill herself, but still that didn't set her free from our marriage.

It went on for years, in that time I didn't touch my wife and I lost my innocence to my childhood love just after our marriage.

One day I heard my wife praying and asking God to set her free from the shameless and non existing marriage and she kind of gave God an ultimatum that she has kept herself for marriage and for the love of her life and now it looks like that will never happen since she is stuck in the loveless marriage with a man who can never notice her since he is in love with another woman, she went on and on and on and at the end she prayed for me to be free and to find a happiness and how she doesn't blame me or hold anything against me since I was forced into this marriage as well.

From that day I began to be restless, I wondered what kind of a woman she is, she kept herself from teenage life right until a marriage and even in marriage of years she never gave up and start going out there to find a lover, that alone humbled my heart, convicted and was just feeling bad.

The feeling went on for a week and I ask myself what kind of answers she is going to get from God, I knew God was eventually going to grant her wish but what if this marriage was never a mistake.

I started to think about our father of faith Abraham, who ask his servant to go and find a wife for his son Isaac, and how Isaac responded to this kind gesture, I read the bible and I learn that Isaac trusted his father as much as his father trusted God, he accepted the gift and he never had a cause to regret it.

The following day I went to visit my father and ask him why did he choose this girl for me to marry and my father said it wasn't because she is from the member of our church, but it was because she is from the family that has the same beliefs and values as ours, I knew that she will be a good wife to you and that will help you be a good husband to her, I saw her as your better half which was going to complete you. However, you have proven me wrong because your marriage is just a shame which left me speechless my father said.

My father continued by saying, the worse of it all is that she has proven to be a good woman whom every man wish to have but not you, she has supported you any every way, even when she was mocked by another woman about your behavior she defended you and kept her honor. Now she doesn't attend most woman meeting because of the shame your other woman is putting her through and she never fought her.

Seriously, God is going to judge me on this my father said, they were families who also wanted her hand in marriage, but I fought to have her as my own daughter in law, me and your mother.

Now I wish I can give her, her own freedom back and her youth back but I can't.

And that day was the 1st day I ever spoke reasonably with my father about my wife, when I got home, I went down on my knees and I prayed to God for direction and help. I ask God to hold on the answered for my wife and give me the chance to learn how to love my wife.

Two weeks later I was so in love with my wife even though I was unable to show it, I 1st went to end my relationship with the other woman, I took a vacation leave at work so that I can meditate on God's word about love and marriage and pray for the love of this good woman in my house.

Eventually God showed me how to love her as he has loved me, my spirit kept on referring me to the story of a man who discovers a treasure in a field and he bought the whole land. And now here we are, I am still guarding this treasure called my wife.

So now is my turn to help my son Bongani to find the love of a good woman, but it looks like is not going to be easy, it looks like he wants to make the same dumb decision I made if not worse.

Then Palesa's father asks how old your son is, they said 26yrs and he said to himself just the right age.

It was a time for Palesa 's father to leave, and then he said his goodbye and left.

Bongani's parents were both in thoughts and eventually Bongani's mother asks her husband, are you thinking what I am thinking? He said I hope so because that will mean is a sign from God that we actually found the perfect woman for our son to marry, she laughed, as it was exactly what she was thinking as well.

The following Sunday they meet with the parents of Palesa at the church after service and they ask if it was possible for them to join them for lunch, Palesa parents agreed, however insisted that they should follow them to their house as they have prepared enough meal.

After a meal Bongani parents reminded Palesa's father of the conversation they had with him about their son.

They ask if it was possible for them to join them in prayer to ask God if it will be his will to join Palesa and Bongani in marriage.

Both parents loved the idea, especially since they are both worried that their children are about to marry the people who has the mark of 666 and they agreed to pray for a week, the following Sunday they had lunch together again

and very one share how the Holy Spirit did not
have any objection to the idea.

Chapter 2

How Bongani and Palesa met

Then the following Sunday they invited both Bongani and Palesa to join them for lunch an after a meal they shared with Bongani and Palesa their desire as parents that they (Bongani and Palesa) should start a courtship and eventually get married.

Bongani and Palesa were shocked by what was said and especially since it was the 1st time they met that day.

The parents explain how their courtship or dating is going to be like. And rules to be followed.

Bongani parents asked him to start visiting Palesa at her house as the kind of courtship they are going to engage into as not the same as the world dating. They ask Bongani to pass by Palesa house for dinner every day as that will help Palesa to learn the roles of being a wife.

And Palesa parents asked Palesa to move back home and travel from home to attend her lecture at that time Palesa was staying in a flat nearby university and also Bongani he was staying at the flat with his girlfriend.

Palesa and Bongani both looked at their parents with a look of disbelieve of what has just been said.

Bongani ask them are you people serious?

Before the parents could answer Palesa said, there is no way they are serious, actually there is no way in hell this is going to happen.

Meanwhile, parents kept quiet so that Palesa and Bongani will express their shock.

Palesa will murmur to herself while Bongani was laughing out loud.

Parents remain silent, observing the reaction of both their children.

Then they spoke and laid down the rules and the process on how this exercise will be executed,

They instructed Palesa to ensure that she is always home in time to welcome Bongani home and wash and massage his feet everyday and also prepare dinner for him. Which means hence forth Bongani will start to have dinner with Palesa family after work.

Bongani was told that he should pass by Palesa house every day after work, and the only day he is free on Saturday and Sunday after church both families will have lunch together.

Bongani attempted to leave the table and his father called him to order, fortunately for both parents both their children have learned the value of respect for their parents so they obeyed their parents' suggestion, however, in their heart individual has a plan to rebel and make every effort to prove that they are not meant for each other.

On Monday Bongani was reminded not to dare them and do as he pleases, it was difficult for him to change his routine just like that, indeed, he resisted for like 2 weeks, the thought of going to visit some girl everyday just because his parent said so, it was ridiculous to him.

However, his parents were determined to see him visiting Palesa as agreed or told.

Palesa as well has sworn never to touch the feet of a man she doesn't know or even like, she resisted too even on the days Bongani came.

After 3 months Bongani and Palesa got tired of their parents nagging and began to do as they were asked.

Palesa began to learn how to cook dinner for a husband and also to welcome her husband to be and massage and wash his feet and her mom was there to teach her how to take a good care of her husband.

Palesa's mom was the kind of woman who has a special touch and every day since she married her husband, she was always giving her husband a massage, she called it a technique to warm a man's heart. She told Palesa that the world believes the way to a man's heart is through his stomach. However, she believes the way to warm a man's heart is through massage, she told Palesa that most men work hard for their family to such extend that they became physically and mentally exhausted, and most men don't want to trouble their spouse with work stress everyday that's why sometimes you find a man in a pub during the week, they believe that if they can have a beer or two they will unwind the stress before they get home and that exposes them to those small girls who want to catch them and destroy their marriage. But if you treat your man with a massage trust me all he is going to think of after a long day at work is to look forward to the relax feeling he will get when you toned down all the stress and the tension caused by work stress and financial challenges. Sometimes you don't even have to say anything when you massage him, just allow his mind to relax and listen to your rhythm of muscle.

Everyday Palesa was taught how to prepare dinner for Bongani and also how to welcome him home. Her mom told her even if you can be a working mom and wife, don't pursue your career at the expense of your marriage make time to be a wife to your husband.

So Palesa took her mom teaching seriously as she needed a successful marriage, every day she will welcome Bongani at the door and walk with him to the living room as he sat down in a living area to relax, she will come with her massage kit and start her duty, at 1st she couldn't do it but was forced to do it and learn how it perfectly with love and eventually she found her way.

After a month she began to do it right and started connecting with the senses of Bongani. And because of that her heart began to warm up for a Bongani.

However, because Bongani girlfriend, Bongani was becoming more and more stubborn, he will come late and moody sometimes, but Palesa was told not to complain and not to pay attention to Bongani behavior but do what she has to do. Her mom told her that in a marriage, we don't do the right thing because our husband has done something to deserve it or we are in the best mood, but we do it because it is our duty and responsibility and we also do it with love even though we receive no love or respect.

After a while Palesa find herself falling for Bongani, she will cook his favorite meal and cook it nicely and also take extra lessons for massages, she also bought the best chair for him to sit on so that she can massage his back without undressing him.

She will begin to wait by the balcony in anticipation of Bongani, looking towards the direction he usually drives through and she will run to open a gate for him and welcome him from his car and carry whatever it is in his hands and walk him to the living area, even though she didn't talk, Bongani could notice the spark in her eyes everytime she looks at him and that infuriated Bongani because he didn't feel the same way, he was still dating the other girl. To him Palesa was still a project to prove his parents wrong.

One day he fell sick and didn't go to work neither did he come for dinner, but his mother later around 7pm informed Palesa of his sickness. Palesa drove her father's car that night to go and see Bongani on his sick bed, getting there she prepared a soup and helped Bongani to eat, I mean this girl actually fed Bongani and nurtured him for 3 days, she didn't even went to her lecture so that she can spend the day with Bongani. After a few days Bongani was fine ready to go to work and she went back home.

A few weeks later it was her birthday and is so happen that it was on Friday, Bongani on that Friday didn't call her and he didn't even come to her house because he went out with his girlfriend on a weekend away.

Palesa waited with anticipation to see what kind of a gift he will buy for her and in fact she was just fantasizing about a romantic day with Bongani.

Unfortunately her dream was shattered badly when she sees that Bongani is nowhere to be found even on Saturday.

On Sunday Bongani just came for lunch as usual with his parents and he didn't even mention anything to Palesa, shame poor Palesa was heartbroken, the worst part was when Bongani mother asks her how was your weekend away with Bongani as she overheard Bongani making arrangement for a weekend getaway.

Palesa now realized that Bongani didn't just forget her birthday, he didn't care, he even opt to take his girlfriend out on that weekend as if he wanted to spite her.

On that table, she broke in tears, now parents realized that Palesa has actually and very badly fallen for Bongani however Bongani is still adamant and insensitive towards her.

Palesa asked to be excused from the table, but since one of the rules was, no one is allowed to leave the table before they finish their meal, her request was denied and that made her feel very worse she felt they were hard on her but they couldn't do or say anything about Bongani spending a weekend away with another girl. She felt betrayed by all of them.

Once everyone was done, she ran to her room and cry even worse and now it was so clear that she is heartbroken. Her mom followed her to her room, she asks her mom how come she hates her so much, why would her own mother be part of a conspiracy to destroy her life and bring pain into her life. She cried and cried and admitted that she is now in love with a man who is not hers and who will never be hers and who doesn't notice or even appreciate her. She said never once since this whole thing started did Bongani appreciated her in anything he doesn't even look at her like he is looking at someone he might marry one day. She continued by saying sometimes I don't even feel like a full woman or beautiful anymore.

He has managed to make me feel insecure and ugly, he is the only man whom I spend most of my day with but still he can't even make one flirty comment, she said to her mom.

Down in the dining room Bongani father is trying to reprimand Bongani and Bongani went outside and take a call and is so happen that he stand right next to the window of Palesa bedroom and Palesa can hear everything he is saying.

Bongani on the call he told the caller that his father is forcing a dead wood down his throat in the name of marriage, which he actually called Palesa a dead wood, wow how cruel and insensitive this man is.

When Palesa heard him she looked at her mom who happened to have heard the same thing Bongani was saying.

Palesa's mother went downstairs and called all parents and she cancelled the dessert and out of shame Bongani's mom agreed because they heard and they could see how bad Palesa is feeling.

Parents also agreed to stop the whole thing as it has been months and Bongani is still adamant and now he is causing pain to Palesa and they prayed and surrender all in the hands of God as they felt that they have failed and also feel like they might have been wrong.

Chapter 3

Palesa grief caused her to fall sick

That night Palesa was attacked by a very bad fever. And around same time something just snaps on Bongani, he began to feel restless and rehearsing so much of all Palesa has shown to him, how he couldn't resist her touch and he is always looking forward to her massage every day, how her kind gesture made him feel good about himself, how his aggressive and negative attitude disappeared and how she was today, he began to feel bad about how he treated her. He couldn't sleep, his feet were very cold and he remembered the nice massages of Palesa and how she makes him feel warm and relaxed, he longed for Palesa's touch of love and care, the whole night it was as if he is feeling the same pain Palesa was feeling that night meanwhile Palesa was rushed to the hospital and was admitted.

Chapter 4

Palesa in hospital

Palesa in hospital got worse, and the more she gets worse the more Bongani is restless and feeling suffocated, like and anxiety attack, he felt like that throughout Monday and Tuesday morning around 6pm on Tuesday Bongani's father received a call from Palesa father to inform him that he won't be able to attend their meeting as Palesa has been admitted in hospital.

It was only then Bongani attacks stop as he overheard his father's conversion, he took his keys and rush to the hospital where Palesa was admitted.

Getting there, he introduced himself as Palesa husband to the nurse, the nurse escort him to Palesa's room getting there he found the Doctor and again, he introduced himself as Palesa's husband, the Doctor told him everything about Palesa condition and it was bad. Bongani fell down on his knees and began to pray in tongues for Palesa as the Doctor was still in the room. By then Palesa parents were coming back from the hospital kitchen, they were shocked to find Bongani by Palesa hospital bed and praying however they didn't say anything to him.

He went on like that the whole night praying by the side of Palesa' s bed, around 6am when the Doctor come surprisingly Palesa has recovered faster than they thought.

He continues to be with her again the whole day on Wednesday around 7pm Palesa regain consciousness and she was surprised to see Bongani by her bed and she got so upset and she asks her parents and the Doctor to never allow Bongani come near her. Bongani wasn't surprised by her reaction, he peacefully went outside, but never left the hospital, he went into the chapel and begin to ask God forgiveness and also asking God to help to win the love of Palesa back as he now realized that she is more than wife for him, he called her "my perfect Rib" he confesses to God that he is in love with Palesa and it will only take the grace of God for him to win her back considering what transpired on Sunday.

After prayer Bongani came back and set outside Palesa room the whole night on Thursday.

By Friday morning Palesa miraculously she was fully well, but still weak, the Doctor discharged her.

Chapter 5

Bongani battle to win Palesa love continued

At home Palesa ask again that Bongani shouldn't be allowed to come close to her, even after she was told about all Bongani efforts at the hospital, to her that was just the action of a remorseful man and she was never going to confuse those feelings with love and her parents agreed that it might not be love but pity.

That made things worse for Bongani however, he was determined to win her back is it was truly love.

Bongani began to pray for hours every day, even when he was at work, and on his own he continue to pass by Palesa house because his heart longed to see Palesa, even though he wasn't welcome, he persisted for a month, after that he called a meeting between his father and Palesa father and poured out his heart to them and ask them to join him in prayer to win back the woman they found for him as this wasn't a mistake as everyone thinks but the will of God for their life, it just took too long for him to realized it and he is not going to accept that it is too late. The man agreed to join him in prayer so that God can touch Palesa to love him again and also to create opportunity to come to Palesa house as he used to join them for Sunday lunch.

It was about the same time when the marriage of Palesa sister Rose was also going through challenges as Bongani came to see Palesa he will find the Rose Palesa sister, crying because of the things her husband is doing outside, Bongani will sit with her and began to counsel her and pray with her.

Chapter 6

The revelation of the miracle of water turning into wine

Bongani asks Rose and said Rose do you still remember the First miracle Jesus performed?

Rose said yes, he turns water into wine, and Bongani asks do you know why he did that, Rose said for the wedding celebration to continue to be fun and also to save the face of the bride and groom.

Bongani said not so if that was the only reason he could allow the master of ceremony to declare that they came to the end of the celebration dismiss everyone, but I think Jesus did that to show that he is the Lord who control time and also he can renew their marriage and sustain their love and made the best love they never enjoy since they were together, to me it meant that if I have a problem in my marriage. I don't have to go to court and ask for the master of court or a judge to declare my marriage finished and issue me with a divorce decree. To me it means if I think I have fallen out of love with my spouse all I have to do is to call on Jesus to renew my love to my wife and that also means from that day I don't have to depend on my effort to make my marriage to work or my wife do's and don'ts. I will depend on him to give us the best love and marriage ever like that best wine Jesus made in the wedding they say it was the best wine of them all. Rose looked at him and for a while she wandered is this the insensitive Bongani I heard so much about, because that day Bongani had encountered the spirit of God and allow God to teach him about love, while Rose was wallowing in thought he said Rose go and think about this and ask God to give you a new wine for your marriage as the one you had prepared has run out, before you go to ask for a master of ceremony declares that the wedding ceremony has come to the end and get a divorce.

Bongani also visited Mike, Rose husband and engage with him about the role of God in their marriage, Mike confide in him that he love Rose but he doesn't know how to be in love with her all the time, how he doesn't know how to be committed to her only and to have self control when it come to other women.

Chapter 7

Revelation of the story of Samaritan woman in marriages

Bongani asks Mike and say do you know why Jesus had to meet a Samaritan woman.

Mike looks at him strangely and in his mind he was thinking what kind of a question is this and how is it related to what I just told him about my inability to have self-control and my sexual habits, but he answered and say I guess Jesus wanted to recruit her to be one of his evangelists so that she can stop hopping from one man to the other.

And Bongani said partially yes, you are right, but why the issue of marriage/husband was the center of their conversation but not living in sin.

Mike said I don't know.

Bongani said to me on the marriage part, it means Jesus was aware that the reason why this woman never held on to one man. It is because of a dissatisfaction. She encounters as the relationship grows and she fell out of love with the man and leave to find another man, and only to experience the same thing with all the man until she met Jesus the man above all man and her love for him made him the last man she ever encounter he gave her the everlasting love she always longed for in all her failed marriages with the husbands she had before, the love that never end but grow stronger and stronger as life goes, Jesus quenched the thirst in her of longing for a better man. Jesus didn't see a loose woman no he saw a dissatisfied woman.

Mike said we are only human there is no way we can measure up to Jesus no one can so I guess the broken relationship are inevitable because people fall in love now only to fall out of love later, that's why you see many get so many girlfriends and cheat all the time this is the case we are cursed with it so the best thing is to never get married because you will be saving yourself a lot of problems.

Bongani looked at him with a shocking face and said so this is it so you sleep with this woman after that you dump her and go to the next woman later you dump her you continue with this vicious circle.

And Mike said if you look at it on one side you will see it that way, but from my experience whenever I got tired of a woman I always discover that she feel the same way she just didn't want to call it quits.

Then Bongani said so that means Samaritan woman was lucky to meet someone like Jesus who was able to save her from changing a man. So would you like to be as lucky as she was?

Mike said what do you mean?

Bongani said everything Jesus did, he was and he is still doing it for our benefit, Jesus was aware of this vicious circle of love web but he didn't want it to continue so he chose the perfect example in the circle and give her what she longed for in all her failed marriages and she went and told another man and woman about the man who was able to give her what she longed for in all her failed marriages. So they followed her because they can associate themselves with her, they were also suffering from the curse of failed marriages and a broken relationship and needed help and they got it.

Bongani said, we need to go to Jesus who saved them and drink this everlasting love for our marriages and relationship, there is no need to make the best out of the bad situation.

We can drink from the best wine and living water Jesus had prepared for this situation and enjoys the everlasting love with our spouse.

So Mike, me and you we can ask Jesus to fill us with this everlasting wine for love and also teach us how to love our wives.

Look at this example where God through Paul spoke about the foundation of marriage and the role of man in the marriage.

God said we should love our wives as Christ loved us. So how did Christ love us, by dying for us, by healing the sick, by feeding the thousands of men who followed Him. When Christ meets a demon possessed people he didn't judge them harshly he understood who was behind their violent behavior. He delivered them, when a woman was brought before him because she was accused of adultery what did he do, by law, he was supposed to stone her instead he protected her by calling out the sins of her accuser. He said he who is without sin, let him cast the 1st stone and no one was found without sin and when they were all gone, he showed the woman his love for her and since that day that woman never committed that sin again. My brother, God's love overcomes everything, if we love our wives by God's love, not by this touching, feeling which are self-centered, trust me nothing will be too hard in our marriage, so me and you now we need to ask God, his love and his way of love for our wife's, I don't know about you, but I am going to fight for Palesa, and I know that through God who is the author and the finisher of this love I am going to win her back because the bible says I can do all things through Christ who strengthen me.

God said in Isaiah whenever we need something we should ask for it, be it loves, wisdom, understanding or anything and in the book of John, God said whatever we ask in his name he will give it to us so that his name may be glorified.

Do you think is God who is glorified by all this broken marriage, fatherless children, court full of divorce cases and all this talk that marriage is overrated, a failing institution, nor is the devil.

God finishes what he has started and also protect it against the gates of hell, all those married couples taking lesson from comic books and pornographic movies on how to make the marriage work, and they have all forgotten that marriage is from God.

It was never a man's idea, but God's. That's why they fail and keep on producing offspring that will fail in their marriage just like them as no one is giving them a chance to go to the roots of this marriage.

So me and you my brother, let's make a vow now that we are going to consult the source for our marriage and he will direct our steps and show us how to love our wife's and have everlasting love.

So from that day Mike joined Bongani in prayer and Mike became a changed man, even Rose confesses that in their life she never saw Mike so loving, so humble and understanding and on Sunday Rose moved back home with Mike and they become a family again.

By then Palesa also has begun to do her part of welcoming Bongani with a foot massage when he gets home and also cooking dinner for him. Rose was doing the same for Mike and Mike confessed to Rose that before, after a long day at work he often had a desire to pass by the bar and drink his sorrow out before he come home but now all he thinks of is how her message takes away all the tension caused by work stress. Her messages are helping him to breathe again, and be ready to face the world again and at work because the previous stress was gone, he was able to face them positively and that helps him to have a good attitude for his work which has lead him to be the best staff member and consequently he was trusted with bigger responsibility which can be said is a promotion with a bigger salary. Now no more money worries because now what I earn I don't split it between my wife, children, another woman and alcohol. So I feel like the king of the universe and this is only the beginning, Mike said.

Is over a year now and Palesa birthday is coming again.

Palesa prayed that if Bongani is really in love with her, he will propose to her on her birthday and this time he will do things differently.

She never mentioned to anyone but to God in prayer.

Bongani and Mike planned for Palesa birthday outing for the whole family that include Bongani parents, Palesa parents Mike and Rose at Hulala lake lodge.

So they also planned Bongani proposal to Palesa there. And it comes to pass, that at the lake the man planned was that after breakfast while sitting and playing games by the pool Bongani will propose.

Chapter 8

Bongani proposed

However, he didn't get the nerve to do it and waited until they were on the boat and he held her hand and pull her towards her father and he went down on his knees and ask for Palesa hand in marriage to her father, he said Dad if you may find me worthy to be your son in law permitted me to marry your daughter Palesa whom has become the center of my life, my joy and my sister in the Lord. I promised to be kind, faithful and loving to her as Christ is to me, I will provide for her when she is in need, pray for her healing when she is sick and protect her when she is under attack as Jesus has done for me. Dad, I promised she will not have a course to be sad or lose her faith me or with God. Through this journey of finding the love I have learned so much and my faith in God has grown I now know who I am in Christ and what is my role as a husband to my wife.

As Bongani was kneeling down Palesa also joined him by kneeling down before her father even though Bongani never ask her to or even told her his plan, by just holding her hands, he took a lead and she followed and that was noticed by everyone on the boat as that was unexpected even other guest noticed the obedience Palesa showed to Bongani she allowed him to lead and she was happy to follow.

The Palesa's father said to his daughter do you promised to obey, respect and love him as your head, your husband as you would do for the Lord Jesus Christ, Palesa said yes, Father, I promised to love and respect Bongani as the bible spoke about Sarah the mother of Grace when she love and obeyed her husband Abraham.

That taught everyone on the boat and her Father turned Palesa and made her face Bongani and he took her left hand and hand it over to Bongani as a sign of his approval to their marriage and said Bongani my son it is giving me a great pleasure to hand over my Palesa to you as your wife. He asks Bongani's father who was already at the right hand side of his son to take hold of Palesa right hand, which also the symbol of passing over the fatherhood of Palesa to him Bongani's father and said I give to you my daughter who is now your daughter by marriage to your son and as Bongani's father accepted Palesa right hands that became the sign that he welcome her into the family. He is now taking the responsibility of a father to Palesa and Bongani's mom was standing on the left side of Bongani as Bongani accepted the left hand of Palesa with both his hands, that was a sign that I accept her as my wife and I will treasure her and hold her tied with both hands and Bongani's mom hands covers the top and the bottom hands of her son who was holding on to Palesa left hands which was a sign to show that me Bonganis mom I will not let this marriage to drop and neither will I allow anything outside to disrupt this marriage. And all of this was revealed to the Pastor who happen to be on a weekend outing with his wife, they were on board as well; he began to speak in tongues and walking towards the couples without an invitation. And ask them to hold on the way they were standing. He began to pray for them by saying yes, father it is as you have purposed and proposed, their hands are all the confirmation of your words that he has accepted the responsibility of the father to this new daughter and also she will never allow this marriage to drop, the Pastor said this as the confirmation of God to Palesa's father who has all this in his mind, but didn't spoke why he was putting those hands like that and also confirming what was on Bongani's mom as to why she was putting her hands around Bongani and Palesa like that, wow it was like they are taking the marriage vows.

That was a sign that everything was led by the spirit of God and the Pastor involvement was God put his signature on the marriage certificate of Bongani and Palesa.

Now Palesa has a new mother, a new father and the man who represents the love of Christ to her for a husband.

In Christ Jesus my righteousness.